MAKING ACCOUNTABLE DECISIONS

OTHER BOOKS BY SAM SILVERSTEIN

The Success Model

No More Excuses

Nonnegotiable

No Matter What

The Lost Commandments

MAKING ACCOUNTABLE DECISIONS

A JOURNEY TO AN ACCOUNTABLE LIFE

WITH BONUS CONTENT FROM

NO MATTER WHAT

BY SAM SILVERSTEIN

SOUND WISDOM
P.O. Box 310
Shippensburg, PA 17257-0310

For more information on publishing and distribution rights, call 717-530-2122 or e-mail info@soundwisdom.com.

Quantity Sales. Special discounts are available on quantity purchases by corporations, associations, and others. For details, contact the Sales Department at Sound Wisdom.

ISBN 13 TP: 978-1-640950-14-6
ISBN 13 eBook: 978-1-640950-15-3

For Worldwide Distribution, Printed in the U.S.A.

Cover/jacket design by Geoff Silverstein
Interior design by Terry Clifton

1 2 3 4 5 6 7 8 / 21 20 19 18

Acknowledgments

Sharon Miner, my friend and part of my team, has made tremendous contributions to this project. Thank you for your thought, care and energy.

I also want to thank David Wildasin and the entire team at Sound Wisdom. Your support of our message on accountability and the work we do enables us to continue to write and impact lives in a powerful way. You are all so important to my team and myself. Thank you!

Decisions Matter

We become what we become because of what we believe and the decisions we make. Our beliefs drive our decisions, and our decisions dictate our results and the legacy we leave. There is a certain definitiveness about a decision that sets you going on a movement forward.

Like it or not, throughout our lives, we are constantly faced with the responsibility of making a decision. There is no escaping this responsibility. Not deciding what to do or how to act in a given situation is, in itself, a decision. It is always easier to make a decision when we know what we believe and what we are trying to achieve.

Making decisions also means accepting the idea that we are part of a bigger picture. We are not alone in our decisions. Our decisions affect not only ourselves, but also the people around us. Our decisions shape our actions. Our actions are received and interpreted by those around us. These actions shape the opinions and feelings of those individuals and, ultimately, the actions they take for or against us. Our decisions determine our legacy.

To a great extent, our beliefs about ourselves and our own capabilities, as well as how we see the world and the forces at play in it, affect what we find possible. These beliefs impact our decisions.

Our decisions not only affect us today, but they also affect our abilities and our decisions in the future. For instance, if you feel out of control in a given situation, you may decide to withdraw or avoid the problems at hand. This decision will lead you to escape from a challenge instead of confronting and possibly overcoming it. The degree to which you avoid or escape problems today impairs your ability to face, deal with, and grow from various challenges in the future. The decisions you make today will prepare you for the decisions you will be faced with tomorrow. As the complexity of life evolves, one decision will build on another, enabling you to handle increasingly difficult situations.

An awareness of the need to decide is the first step toward growth. It is critical that we understand the importance of our decisions and also the value of the present. By focusing on our current actions and living in the moment, we develop a certain mindfulness and can apply ourselves to do the very best job possible right now! Clarity of mind allows us to recognize the decisions at hand and deal with them in a positive and proactive manner.

When we choose to focus our decisions on those things that we can control, we will get a result. When we focus on what we cannot control, there will be fewer or even no choices, and so we will be unable to make a decision that can move us forward. In any situation, the question at hand is, "What can I control in this moment?" When you ask and answer that question, you will know where to focus your thoughts and creative powers. You will find yourself making decisions that can have a tremendous impact on your ability to move forward.

Some decisions are easy to make, and others are more difficult. Understanding the possible outcomes helps you make some of those decisions.

As you read this book, you will encounter principles that will help you make accountable decisions. Each axiom is followed by a story that illustrates the respective principle, along with one or more clarifying paragraphs. In the clarifying paragraphs, you will find statements of belief and, often, additional questions. It is not my intention to provide you with answers based on my belief system but rather to offer questions that will allow you to probe deeper into your thoughts and feelings.

On the pages following the statements and clarifying paragraph, you will find action ideas and questions to take you on a deeper discovery of your beliefs, options, opportunities, and ultimately your decisions.

I would like to encourage you to read through the entire book. Then, return to the first of the statements and focus on the questions and action ideas for a week before moving on to the next one. If you only spend five minutes each morning thinking about that one area, at the end of the week you will have invested 35 minutes in yourself by giving meaningful thought to a specific, important area of your life. You will see amazing transformation in what you think and do.

Many of the decisions we face have multiple options. Sometimes we are dealing with right and wrong, but many times there is no wrong answer. The brevity I take in expanding on each decision is by design. It is my goal to assist you in starting the process. You must then accept the responsibility to probe deeper and reach your true inner feelings, desires, and beliefs. You must make these decisions for yourself.

It is a journey we all take, building one decision upon another as we grow, prosper, and shape our legacy. You can create the future you desire based on the decisions you make today!

If It Is Important to You, It Is Valuable to You

Have you ever misplaced something that you absolutely had to find? The agony of having your whole world come to a halt until you find it can become overwhelming. For me, I become obsessed with locating something I have lost. It could be something that I have not used for several days, weeks, or even months, but when I need it, I need it.

I may not wear a watch for several days, but I want to know where my watch is and that it is running and safe. I want to know that when I need it, it will be there.

It is generally not until it is needed that I realize how important and valuable something may be. That is how most things are in life. Their value is not noticed unless they benefit us. The most important things in our personal and professional life cannot be measured in dollars and cents. "Things" may be fun, and they may be nice to have, wear, or play with; but what is really important is almost always attached to a relationship, and relationships are with people.

Our lives can be greatly enhanced by taking the time to determine what is important to us. If people are important to you, then tell them. Let them know that they mean a lot to you, that you appreciate them, and that you value having them in your life. Let those people know the impact they have on you and how your life is better because they play a role in it.

What is important to you has value to you. So often we say that certain things are important, but we discover that they are not important; they are just what is screaming the loudest at that moment in time. Determine what is really important to you, and let go of the things that are unimportant.

What is really important to you?

What actions do you take that align with what you say is important?

What You Believe about Your Future Will Drive Your Actions Today

A friend of mine, who was an executive director of a leadership organization, had a desire to travel the world and teach leadership. She spoke this desire to her husband one day while they were sitting in their home dreaming about the future.

My friend and her husband, along with their son, made a decision to take a once-in-a-lifetime nine-day family vacation to Hawaii. She had a childhood friend who had invited them to come visit before her friend's husband's tour of duty was up in Hawaii. How could they pass that up?

After returning home from that trip, her friend, who was the highest ranking enlisted Chief Master Sergeant in the US Air Force Chaplain Service, called and invited her to travel the Pacific Rim with the US Air Force to teach leadership to the Chaplain Service. The trip took her to Honolulu, Guam, Japan, and South Korea. My friend's desire to travel the world and teach leadership had become a reality.

Your future is designed first by what you speak and then by what you do, not the other way around. The possibilities of what your future can be are limited only by your creative thoughts. Many times we limit our dreams and aspirations to what we think is possible. When we think anything is feasible, then the possibilities for us change dramatically.

You do not have to know how you are going to achieve your future to actualize it. You only need to see it, want it, and commit to it. I have always found that once I start to pursue something, the "hows" present themselves over time. Just believing that I will figure it out as I go has been very powerful in moving me forward toward my future.

Life is a self-fulfilling prophecy. By opening your mind to the possibilities, you form beliefs that are filled with your desired achievements. This new expanded belief in your future will drive you to do what is necessary today to arrive at the future you create.

Describe what your future looks like.

What steps must you start taking to make that future a reality?

Choose What You Think

My assistant and I had been invited to dinner with the leadership team from the company at which we were presenting the next day. We were looking forward to presenting a program on the importance of accountability to 500 supervisory workers in the energy industry.

About midway through dinner, the conversation turned to the next day's program, and the chief operating officer said to me, "Sam, keep it simple tomorrow. Just give these guys one or two points. After all, they do not have a college degree."

I could tell that my assistant was mustering all the restraint she could to keep from saying something distasteful to the client, and frankly, so was I; but it was neither the time nor the place for that. The next day we presented the stellar program we would present to any organization, and we did not dumb it down.

The problem is not just with what that COO said; it is with the way he thinks. It is impossible for the people he leads to rise to their highest potential because he thinks that their lack of a college degree limits their potential.

My father did not have a college degree, and he was one of the smartest men I have known. Dad wanted to be an astrophysicist, but he could not afford to go to college. Ultimately, my father and mother started and built a successful business. He was able to send all three of his children to college and even graduate school. And yet, he never got his college degree.

What you think about people affects your actions toward them, and your actions will affect your results. If you limit people in your thinking, you will limit their opportunities and possibilities in your actions. A positive thought will produce a positive result.

In any given situation, you get to choose your thoughts. You choose your thoughts when the car in front of you does not go the instant the light turns green. You choose your thoughts when you meet someone and they have tattoos or piercings, or they dress differently than you, or they look differently than you. You choose what to think, and what you think drives what you do, how you react, and ultimately the course you take.

You, and only you, have control over your thoughts. Make it a personal priority to be aware of and focus your thoughts. Actively pay attention to what you think about. Set aside time to focus your thoughts on what is important and what matters. Also, set aside time to think about what you think about.

Do you participate in your thought life, or do you let your mind wander?

Do you spend time paying attention to what you think about?

Choose one area of importance in your life and focus on thinking about it.

Balance

Oftentimes when we think of balance we think of being able to juggle work and home life, family and friends, exercise and food. We think of striking some sort of balance that will keep us at an optimum level of working hard, spending the right amount of time with others, and keeping healthy.

While these elements of life are important, I would like to submit to you that the most important balance to achieve is to stay balanced spiritually. What does it mean to be spiritually balanced? To be spiritually balanced means you are spending time feeding your spirit with wisdom, knowledge, and truth. Strengthen your soul with the core tenets that become the foundation of everything you believe.

Recently, I took the time to go on a retreat for four days. At this retreat we had no electronics and we were totally silent from 9:00 P.M. until 1:30 P.M. the next day. There were no phone calls, no text messages, no e-mails, no televisions, and no newspapers. It was a powerful time to listen to my inner voice without any distractions.

Any time I have moved into a new home with empty closets, I have wondered how long those spaces would remain empty. Over time, we fill all the available space in our homes, and it can become cluttered. The same thing can happen within us as people.

When you eliminate the clutter and actively work to create space in your mind and in your heart for things to happen, you have the opportunity for that space to be filled with something meaningful.

I came away from that experience with a deeper understanding of what my purpose is in this life. I not only took time to work on my physical body, but I took time to cultivate my spiritual side as well.

Do you balance the physical and spiritual sides of your life? Do you take care of your physical being as well as feed and nurture your spiritual side? Balance in the two areas leads to fulfillment, contentment, and personal growth. Balance comes out of what you believe, and it always starts with knowing what you believe.

What can you do so that one area of your life does not suffer because of imbalance?

Choose Virtue

As an author, I love to look up the definition of words from the *Webster's 1828 Dictionary*. The original meaning of words and how their definitions have changed over the years amazes me.

In this dictionary, the word *virtue* is defined as nothing but "voluntary obedience to the truth."[1] We live in a time in which people struggle with determining what constitutes truth. I still believe there is right and wrong, truth and lies, moral excellence and righteousness. Unwritten principles dictate that true success and happiness do not come from impure thoughts or actions.

When we have good thoughts, good things get produced. Our relationships are better both professionally and personally. Living a positive virtuous life is a choice.

As human beings, we are gifted with the ability to choose. We really do have the responsibility to make so many choices, not only in the physical aspects of our life, but in the intellectual, emotional, and spiritual areas as well. We all get to choose where we live in our thought life. We get to direct our thoughts and determine the course that we allow our minds to follow.

---

1 *Webster's 1828 Dictionary* (1828), s.v. "virtue," http://webstersdictionary1828.com/Dictionary/virtue.

> Whatever things are true, whatever things are noble, whatever things are just, whatever things are pure, whatever things are lovely, whatever things are of good report, if there is any virtue and if there is anything praiseworthy—meditate on these things.[1]

Through kindness in attitude and actions, you grow as an individual and increase your personal power. Virtuous living creates enormous power. The virtue you display will attract others like a magnet!

1 Phil. 4:8 NKJV.

For the next seven days, write down the steps you can take to better live a virtuous life.

Respect Others

It has been said that variety is the spice of life. I believe that is true. But more importantly, I believe it is true about the people with whom we surround ourselves.

We are creatures of habit. So often we assemble with people who are just like us, and we do not allow ourselves the honor of getting to know people of different races, ethnicities, and socioeconomic status.

I have learned to respect others by taking the time to get to know other people. I have made an effort to get to know people who do not look like me or live where I live or participate in the activities in which I normally participate. There is an amazing richness of humanity. We have the opportunity to get to know if only we would take the time and make the effort.

Take the time to get to know someone who does not look like you. You might find you have a lot in common, and respect for each other is something you might share. You will learn something along the way. You may find someone to whom you will be able to bring value. And you may discover someone who will add value to your life, be there for you, and become a dear friend.

Unfamiliarity can be a scary thing. I am reminded of a story of a woman who was on a Korean Air flight coming from Seoul, South Korea, back to Hawaii. On the flight she was seated next to a couple with a young child who was about 18 months old. They did not speak English, and she did not speak Korean; but by the end of the flight she was holding their baby. When they departed, there were no words spoken—just a warm embrace. It is our humanity that we have in common.

By honoring others you honor yourself. Respect for others is translated into empowerment of others. Empowered people achieve excellence. Respect for others is a supreme compliment.

How do you respect someone you do not like?

Respect Yourself

Respect is one of those qualities that can be hard to define. Everybody wants it, but sometimes it is hard to give. I had the opportunity to witness an exchange of respect between two people in a unexpected setting, and it was beautiful.

While touring a state prison, the warden I was with noticed an inmate had not properly taken the time to shave his facial hair. This inmate had apparently been warned about his facial hair once before. In front of my assistant and myself, the warden, with great respect, corrected the inmate. There was not any devaluing in either direction. There was only complete respect.

It was clear to us at that moment that the warden had created an environment where respect for yourself was important. Respect for your appearance, respect for your speech, and respect for how you treat people mattered. When the warden showed respect for the inmate and the inmate showed respect for the warden, an environment of respect was established. It is in this environment that the inmate could discover respect for himself.

This may have been the first time that someone spoke to the inmate with respect. This may have been the first time that the inmate felt that way about himself. That self-respect could have a profound impact on his decisions in the future.

The warden not only had a standard of respect that she choose to live out in her life, but she also modeled respect as an example for everyone who worked in the prison as well as the inmates who were housed there. It was a powerful position to take, and her actions helped teach so many other people how to embody respect also.

Respect for yourself means nurturing, protecting, and empowering your spiritual and physical being. By respecting yourself, you can better respect others. You have to believe that you are important and that you matter. You have value because you are a human being—no more and no less than the value placed on a prince or princess.

How do you provide yourself with the nurturing necessary to grow and flourish?

Keep Life's Issues in Perspective

Have you ever considered that everything has a purpose? Learning to live life with purpose and intentionality will give us a perspective that will help us better navigate the challenges and opportunities in life. When we know our purpose, then life's issues do not become as much of a distraction. When we know why we do what we do, we are better able to stay on course in the face of challenges.

Purpose requires thought and paying attention to what is going through your head. Your decisions are made on purpose, with purpose, and for a purpose.

Have you ever driven somewhere, and when you arrived, you did not even remember how you got there? You did not remember if there were any red lights, if you stopped, or which streets you took? It can be the same way in our life. We get "stuff" done at home or at work, and the weeks roll by. There have been times in my life where I "woke up" and discovered that I was just going through the motions. I was getting up, going to work, working, coming home, and then going to bed.

It is so important to slow things down and to take the time to think about our lives, what we want to experience, what we want to accomplish, and who we want to become. We should do the same thing at work and think about who we want to become professionally and how we want to impact the organization at which we work. This is about taking the time to discover your gifts and to understand your purpose. Then you are able to bring purpose to everything you do.

When we take the time to be purposeful, then events start to happen for a reason. But we must also understand that there are some events that we cannot influence. They do not happen because of us, but they affect us. When we accept those events, even embrace them, we can incorporate decisions around them in the same way that we make decisions around the events in our life that we can control.

Once we are living with purpose, the events of our life fall into place. We better understand the connection between one event and another. We also are better positioned to work with life's issues, which are, for the most part, beyond our control.

Do you keep your head about you? Are your decisions based solely on emotion, or is rational thinking involved? Do the little issues get in the way of the big ones? Many times, keeping life in perspective means being able to step "outside" of yourself and look back at your situation with less emotion. What advice would you give someone else in a similar situation? Does this objective advice make sense for you?

When do you find yourself allowing events in your life to impact how you make decisions?

Live with Humility

Living with humility can be a leader's greatest asset because it means that they have spent most of their time with others on their mind. Thinking about other people is critical for a leader because being responsible for the success and safety of other people is the leader's primary responsibility.

I had the great honor of serving as president of the National Speakers Association in 2008. It was a big responsibility leading 3,600 members stateside and being seen as a leader by over 5,000 professional speakers internationally. There was no way I could have done a good job as president without the support of countless others who helped me perform the duties.

Every decision that had to be made was made on behalf of what was best for the members and the organization, and that required me to have the members constantly on my mind. Leadership is a responsibility, and I would never have made it through the year without a team of great people. It was critical to my success as a leader of this organization that I understand that it was the team that made me successful, not the other way around.

When you believe that you alone are responsible for your success, you will devalue your team's participation, diminish their importance to you, and erode the relationship between you and them. When you see the team around you as the critical element in your success, then you respond to them differently. You reward your team differently. You want to help and serve them differently. Ultimately, you will have a different relationship, and future success will come quicker for you all.

To grow and achieve, it is important to place your focus on your vision and your goals. By always looking for credit, you falsely build yourself up at the expense of others. By living a humble life, you build up others. Helping other people achieve success is the greatest reward for the humble person.

How does your ego edge into the words you use and the actions you take?

How can you remove your ego from your communications and relationships?

Be Courageous

I entered a state prison recently, and my mind was racing. Why were all these people here? What had they done? Didn't they know better? Surely this could never happen to me, right? It is very easy to make assumptions about people, their situations, and their choices. Without having all the facts and without having been in their situation, understanding what they have dealt with, we just cannot know why they have made the decisions that they have.

I was not entering the jail as a resident but rather as a guest. The warden had invited me to tour the facility. Not sure what to expect, I was highly engaged as I passed through security and walked through the first locked door. But when I entered a cellblock pod and heard the door close behind me, it all became very real.

The pod that I was being shown at the time was a faith-based, or opt-in, pod. Inside were rows upon rows of bunk beds. Forty-eight prisoners in all were living in this space. A waist-high wall separated the living area from the showers, toilets, and sinks. There was what looked to be a small 19-inch television on the wall. There were a lot of people in a relatively small area. It felt confining.

The warden asked if someone would tell me about the facility, the pod, and what life was like. An inmate named Shane stepped forward and volunteered to share with us. Shane said that he had been married for 18 years but was now divorced. He had owned a large trucking business and at one time had 450 employees. Shane said that he had made a bad decision and that was why he was in prison.

Shane also shared that he felt that being in prison and in this pod was an opportunity to change, to get better. He was emotional as he expressed that he was thankful for being there and for what he was experiencing. He was discovering his faith and gaining clarity about how he wanted to live his life and what he believed. I did not expect him to share that sentiment. I saw the sincere look in his eyes as he spoke to me, and I felt the emotion he shared and immediately felt connected to him. It was a powerful moment.

Shane was being a courageous leader. He stepped up to talk. The first characteristic of leadership is to step up. He did that and did it great. Shane was courageous and transparent. He shared openly about his past, his mistakes, and what he believed. He took responsibility for his actions. He sought to get better. He showed his repentance. He showed his remorse. He showed gratefulness for the opportunity to be in the faith-based pod program. All of this happened in five minutes.

It is easy to expect a "certain" type of person to be in prison. It is easy to categorize prisoners by race or socioeconomic status. This well-spoken man shattered what would be the expectation of many people.

Shane taught me a lot, and that is what leaders do. Leaders are always teaching. They do not necessarily set out to teach, but they do—every single time you are with them. Shane taught me that the courage it takes to step up, admit your faults, and not hide behind false pretenses is the courage that will propel you forward as a person and as a leader. People want to follow courageous leaders.

Shane proves that leadership is not positional. "Inmate" is not directly connected to leadership on any organizational chart. I had myths and stereotypes about what type of people are in prison. I was wrong. People make mistakes. We all do.

What assumptions about people may be holding you back? Do you inspire the people around you? Are you being a Courageous Leader™?

Many times we let our fears get in the way of being courageous. This happens when we focus on what might go wrong that probably will not go wrong. Instead, we need to focus on what our personal gifts are, what possibilities lie ahead for us, and the powerful positive life we really are equipped to create.

Fear of failure and fear of the unknown get in the way of many people's successes. People who are "frozen" by fear do not do what is necessary to achieve what it is they are seeking. If you let fear negatively affect your actions, you are condemning yourself to failure through inactivity. Are you able to control your fears, or do they control you? Do you let anything stand in your way of achieving what you are seeking?

What fears do you have that may be holding you back?

How can you overcome those fears?

What can you do to be more courageous?

Do What You Have to Do until You Get to Do What You Want to Do

Sacrifice is a word that we do not always want to apply to our lives, but for everything worth having there is a cost. Oftentimes we see things that we want but do not want to pay the price. Until we are willing to pay the price it is very unlikely that we can have what we desire.

As a cross-country runner in high school, I, along with all my teammates, dreamed of running the Boston Marathon. After many years away from competitive running, I re-engaged my love of running, began training, and eventually qualified and ran the Boston Marathon.

In order to qualify and run in the marathon, it cost me time, discipline, and physical pain. I arose most mornings by 5:30 A.M., logged 70 miles a week running, and paid strict attention to my diet in order to condition myself to run a fast enough time to qualify and then compete in the race. The price I paid on the front end was worth the reward and satisfaction I received from being a part of this amazing event.

In the process, I chose to give up late nights so I could wake up early. I chose to give up some food I enjoyed in order to be as fit as possible. And I chose to forgo some activities on Saturdays, so I could run the 20- to 24-mile runs necessary to be able to handle the grueling length of the marathon. I did what was necessary in order to get to do what I really wanted to do—run the Boston Marathon!

Do not be afraid to sacrifice instant gratification. We live in a world where the things we want, we want them now. We go into debt to have the things we cannot afford or spend our money on fast food because we do not want to take the time to cook. Both have long-term consequences when we consistently make these choices.

Think about what it is you want to achieve, who you want to become, and the life you would like to live. Then, ask yourself, "What is necessary for me to commit to today so that I can achieve that life tomorrow?" I am not saying that you have to give up everything in your life that you enjoy. I am saying that paying a price today may very well end up feeling like a small price to pay when you achieve your dreams.

There are no overnight successes. What appears to be instant success is usually many months and even years of dedicated work that has built up to eventual success. Do not look for instant gratification. Recognize that if you work hard at what has to be done you will reap the rewards and get to where you want to be.

What do you need to be doing to achieve your dreams?

Be Willing to Make Tough Decisions

Knowing what you believe and value is one of the most important things you can do for yourself.

Just because you say you believe something does not make it truth. If your actions do not support the belief, then it really is not a belief. It is essential to have a clear set of nonnegotiable values that can awaken your own unique, authentic personal power. Those nonnegotiable beliefs are what shape the actions that align with what you say you believe.

When we know what in our life is nonnegotiable, we know where our power and control lie. People who build powerful positive values are not perfect, but they are more likely to have lives that function well and attract others. They are more likely to live lives designed with purpose.

Tough decisions become easier when we know what we believe. When we take the time to say what is nonnegotiable in our life, then what we are doing is making decisions before the situations even present themselves.

One of my values is integrity. I define integrity as: "I make decisions based on the belief that my word is my bond and doing what is right is always the right thing to do. I commit to this no matter what." Like all of us, I find myself in situations where I have to make a decision on how to act or what to do. Maybe I told a friend I would do something or I committed to helping someone with a project. Even when an exciting opportunity comes up, I know that "my word is my bond," and that is a no matter what for me. Decision made!

It is important for you to know your values and to continuously work to incorporate them in all of your decisions. Living your values consistently will help you with both the easy decisions and, most importantly, the tough ones.

Decisions can be difficult. Can you make a tough decision? Many times a decision that is in the best interest of someone else may not be in your best interest. Can you do what is right even if the outcome is not what is best for you? Some decisions are uncomfortable for us as individuals, but we still need to make them.

In what area do you have trouble making decisions?

Strive for Excellence

After every program I present, my assistant and I take time and ask the question, "How can we make it better?" Regardless of how the program was received by the audience, we consistently strive for excellence.

The interesting part is that no matter how long we have been asking that question, we always find an idea or way to improve the program. Sometimes it is something new to try that does not work out, and we go back to the way I did it before. Sometimes we make small changes and they help the overall program. We are constantly asking that question and continually finding ways to improve.

Excellence is a process. It is a mind-set, a way of thinking; a constant goal that is set before you. Excellence is not about perfection. Perfection is a goal we can never obtain. People who strive for perfection find themselves frustrated and never reaching the goal. People who strive for perfection are always waiting for the perfect time to start a project or do something. It is not unusual to see people who strive for perfection underperforming compared to people who strive for excellence.

Please do not misinterpret striving for excellence as not ever being satisfied with what you have. I am always grateful for what I have achieved.

People who strive for excellence always want to get better. To them, excellence is a lifestyle that motivates them to be their very best. When they achieve whatever goal is set before them, they simply set another.

When we strive for excellence, we have made a conscious decision to enter into a process of always getting better at what we do. Being better not only impacts our lives, but it impacts the lives of everyone around us. Striving for excellence sets an example that can inspire others to want to strive for excellence also.

Excellence is a way of thinking. It is not a way of doing. When you strive for excellence, you are not willing to settle for just getting the job done; you want to complete your tasks with a level of quality that goes beyond being simply acceptable.

What beliefs might you have that keep you from performing at a level of excellence in everything you do?

Decide to Seek Knowledge

So often we think of education in terms of stages of life. We are taught that you go through K–12, then, if you can afford it, on to college and maybe even on to graduate studies. But knowledge is readily available to us in today's society through the Internet, the library, PBS, and the millions of books that have been written. Through these outlets we can learn anything we desire.

YouTube teaches us how to build anything, fix anything, bake anything, make anything—you name it. It is endless what we can learn.

I have always been a seeker of knowledge. I have always wanted to learn more about the areas in which I have been interested, like my profession, my hobbies, and people. When I owned a window and door manufacturing business, I learned everything I could about that industry.

Recently, my yearning for knowledge has taken on a new dimension. It has been more of a spiritual path, and along that journey I am finding that my search for knowledge in this area has become much more meaningful. I have begun to thoroughly understand what I truly believe and value. And because of my quest to more deeply understand my values and beliefs, my relationships, my business, and my personal life have been greatly enriched.

When you seek knowledge, you are investing in yourself. Education opens new doors. As you expand your education, you expand your possibilities. Education does not have to be traditional or formal. It can be spiritual, it can be from books you decide to explore, and it can come from the people with whom you surround yourself.

What is your plan for continuous personal learning and development?

Focus on and Meet the Needs of Others

My wife and I have been blessed with four wonderful children who are now successful adults. They are now beginning to marry and bless us with grandchildren. There have been so many birthday parties, and there will be many more to come. Celebrating birthdays is a wonderful way to focus on and meet the needs of others.

My wife always makes every birthday special. She makes each of us feel as if that day was designed just for us. The night before a birthday, my wife would always sit with our children and ask them the best part of the year that had just passed. After they shared their highlights, she would ask them what they saw as possibilities for the year ahead. She made sure the entire birthday celebration had a focus. It was about the individual and helping them to be thankful for what they had.

I never thought celebrating a birthday could be a basic need of an individual. I had always taken a simple birthday party for granted until my wife and I experienced a ministry that gives birthday parties to children who have been removed from their home because of some type of abuse. Many of the children had never had a birthday party. No one ever focused on them or their needs.

It was very humbling to watch these kids be thankful for gifts given to them by total strangers. To watch their face light up because they got what was on their wish list was an experience I never want to forget. You see, some of these children have never been made to feel special, and their needs were always secondary in their house.

Focusing on the needs of others and seeking their success is a gift from you to them. The impact you have on their life is significant, and the impact they will have on the lives of the people around them is immense.

How important is the success of those around you? Do you spend time helping others achieve success? Helping others is a reward in and of itself. And in the end, you may find that by helping other people achieve their goals, they may want to help you achieve yours.

What does it mean to focus on the needs of others?

How can you better serve the needs of the people in your life?

Let People Stand on Their Own Merit

My assistant has a very diverse set of people with whom she regularly interacts. From senior citizens, to children in the foster care system, to women in recovery, to rich people, to poor people, to people of every color, she calls them all friends. It is incredibly powerful to watch her interact with all these friends, as she speaks to them and treats them all exactly the same—with love, respect, and honor.

I have had the opportunity to meet several of her friends and was struck by a young man whom I might not have noticed or had the time for a few years back. His life story is not hidden. It is written all over his body in tattoos. There was a time in my life when I would have judged him as someone who was not worthy of my time and attention.

This young man shared a moving story with me. Learning about his challenges and how he overcame them taught me that all people have things in common. We all face challenges. They may simply be different challenges. Just because someone looks different does not mean they are less than or more than.

Getting to know this young man changed me and my indifference to people who do not look like me, come from the same socioeconomic background, or believe what I believe. How I see people, open up to people, and embrace people has been forever altered. This young man is smart, entrepreneurial, and, like all of us, he wants to matter and be successful. His merit is not determined by how he looks or an unfair judgment that I may make.

One of the main reasons people fail is that they prejudge whether a person can or cannot do something. Does someone's clothes, looks, or residence really tell something important about them? Does sex, race, or creed really make a difference in someone's ability to perform a certain task?

How do you treat people? If you are a minority, how would you like to be treated? Your actions and statements need to affirm your belief of equality. Do not pass up opportunities by prejudging the outcome. Give people a fair chance to produce positive results.

What are the things that are in you that cause you not to treat people equally?

Believe in Yourself

Of all the groups of people to whom I have had the opportunity to speak, the group that has moved me the most is a group of women who are recovering from addiction. These courageous ladies showed me what it means to believe in yourself.

One step they have to take in order to stay clean is to learn how to believe in themselves again, because the sickness of addiction has taken their families, their dignity, and their self-worth. The very successful program these women are in is designed to rebuild their self-image and their self-esteem. The program is designed to let these women know that they have true value as people. The one quality that we all need that is prevalent in their journey is strength.

It takes strength to believe in yourself when everyone around you has given up on you. These women fight the demon of addiction daily, and one of their greatest assets is believing in themselves and that they can stay sober.

We all face the challenges of failure, uncertainty, and weakness. We all have moments when we need to face a situation and make a decision. While it is nice when other people believe in you, it is far more important for you to believe in yourself. This inner strength has the power to guide you through the toughest of situations. Even though you may not know the outcome that lies ahead, believing in yourself allows you to move forward, stay steady, and persist.

Your self-esteem limits or enhances your ability to go through your challenge, whatever it may be, successfully. If you look at yourself as a loser, it is impossible to be a winner. If you have a good healthy self-image, you will have a greater will and ability to succeed. People with good self-images better understand the relationship between their optimal selves and their actual selves and are constantly striving to achieve their higher potential.

How do you see yourself?

What can be done to strengthen your self-esteem?

If you had more self-esteem, what would you be able to accomplish?

Know What You Believe

I was in New York presenting a new program on knowing what you believe and value. The evening before my program, I was invited to a dinner with some of the leaders of the organization. After dinner we had an open discussion about the material I was going to present the next day. The conversation was going quite well, and I felt the group was reaching an understanding of what it means to know what you believe.

I received a question that at the time I struggled to answer. A gentleman who had been participating in and listening to the conversation asked me, "Sam, what do you do if you do not know what you believe?"

I did not know what to say and fumbled for an answer. I left there not having given a genuinely solid answer to his question. I pondered his inquiry for months. It had a profound effect on me. It was important that I have an answer.

Today, I would ask him to think about the things he values in his life and is unwilling to compromise on. I would ask, "What are your foundational values, your relational values, your professional values, and your community values? What is nonnegotiable in your life?"

When you know what you believe, your actions align with your words. Many times it is easy to say what is right. Do your actions agree with your statements? Do you walk your talk, or do you say one thing and do another? Do you expect more from others than from yourself?

When your actions are aligned with your words, you gain credibility. People believe in what you say and are more likely to assist you as you pursue your goals. As your deeds come in line with your words, you will notice a significant increase in your productivity and level of achievement.

When in your life do your actions not align with what you say you believe?

Choose Carefully the Standard by Which You Live Your Life

So often we find ourselves in situations that challenge our faith. At times it may be financial challenges, relational challenges, health challenges, or emotional challenges. And yes, sometimes it is all these things at the same time!

As human beings, in every situation, what we believe determines what our response will be when the challenges come. We go with what we know. We fall back on what we believe. We look for the answers in the standard by which we choose to live our lives.

In the 2014 movie *Hercules,* the main character, played by Dwayne Johnson, and his comrades accept the challenge to turn a group of farmers and merchants into warriors after Lord Cotys's army is destroyed by the enemy, the warlord Rhesus. Hercules and his comrades train the team of misfits by teaching them how to protect Lord Cotys in battle by using the "shield wall."

The shield wall is a battle stance that requires the warriors to plant their feet, lock their shields, and form a human fortress around Lord Cotys. Hercules tells his trainees, "The shield wall shall never break formation. Remember these words and you will taste victory."

This became their standard. This became what they believed and the basis for their decisions. Ultimately, by sticking to their standard, even in the direst of situations—and that is the key—they were able to taste victory. They chose to believe in the shield wall. They were committed to establishing and maintaining that wall at all costs. This was their standard.

You measure your decisions, results, and values based on the standard you have chosen. People will want to associate with you because of who you are and what you stand for. People are naturally attracted to others with similar values.

What is your standard?

How does your standard show up in your life?

Be Generous

People who are generous live out of a mentality of abundance. They have an abundance of three things that make up their generosity: they give of their time, their talent, and their treasure. They look to give their time, talent, and what is important to them freely.

Being generous is more than just giving money to your favorite charity or volunteering at the homeless shelter, which are wonderful things to do. People who are generous have moved past the occasional act of volunteering or giving and have become compulsive about giving of their time, their talent, and their treasure. They cannot help it.

If you have ever met someone who is truly generous, you cannot help but walk away from him or her knowing that you have received something of value. Generous people live out of abundance and because this is the way they think; they believe that they have more than enough. Truly generous people know that it is not about what you get; it is about what you give.

Giving reinforces your faith in what you believe. Giving is an investment in your spirit, your well-being, and other people. Giving always brings returns.

Maybe like me you have noticed that some people, no matter how little they have, always find a way to give something to a good cause or to someone else who may need it more. And there are also those people who, no matter how blessed they are and how much they have, struggle to part with anything. Giving is a way of thinking and being.

Are you always looking to receive? Do you look to give first or to take? It is an unwritten law that you cannot take more than you give. A successful society is built on people giving to others. You may not receive back from those to whom you give, but it will come back in some way. The more you give, the more you will receive. Helping others achieve their success will not only prove to be rewarding, but you will also grow in the process. As you grow, you will find yourself closer to your goals.

How does generosity show up in your life?

How can you do more for others?

Live for Today

People who are in recovery programs have to learn to live in the moment and pay attention to the thoughts that come into their head. They have to learn to participate in their thought life if they are ever going to stay clean.

In order for them to get well, they have to learn to live for today because they are keenly aware that today is really all they have. They know that yesterday is but a memory, tomorrow is just dream, and now becomes a very precious moment in time.

Truth be told, that is all any of us have. What we decide to do in the here and now is what will determine our future. We should plan for the future and remember the past—but not at the expense of living life to the fullest in the present.

My wife and I both have mothers who have memory challenges. Many times when we sit down to eat lunch, they cannot remember what they ate for breakfast. What we have noticed is that when we are with either of them, they really enjoy the time we share. So do we.

It does not matter that they do not remember breakfast. In that moment, all that matters to us and to them is that they are enjoying themselves, enjoying being together, and enjoying the wonderful life moments our family shares with them. Living for today is what we have, and we love every moment of it.

There are some key questions we should ask ourselves every day. What do we do right now? How do we live now? What makes today the best day it can be?

The past is gone. We cannot affect anything that has come before this time. The future inspires our actions today and gives us the energy to do what we must to reach our futures. The present is where we take action and achieve results.

If we dwell on past failures, we lose sight of our vision and our goals. When that happens, the source of our energy today is gone, and we stray off course. Learn from the past. Do not live there. Look to the future. Draw energy from the vibrant picture you paint of what it is you desire, and do today whatever it takes to achieve that vision.

What will you do today to make sure you are living life to the fullest?

Be Happy

No matter what season of life you are in, you can be happy. Being happy is a choice. It is a way of thinking.

If being happy is a choice, then being sad or frustrated or aggravated are also choices. Do you ever notice that some people are always mad and so are usually never fun to be around? Do you know people who are always happy, who always have a kind word, and who are always a joy to be with? Happiness is contagious. When a happy person is around other people, they naturally start to be happy. When someone laughs, we naturally want to laugh also.

I believe there are three things you need in order to make it through any season in life. If you have a word to hang on to, a song to sing, and a friend to talk to, you are going to be okay.

When I was growing up, my dad would always tell us kids as he left the house, "Peace on earth, good will toward men." Dad did not want us kids to be angry with each other or picking fights. He wanted us to be happy, to discover joy, and to enjoy being together. Those words still have meaning for me today, and I am often reminded of my father's words when I need to calm a storm in my life. His words have become my words. I look for the peace and focus on being happy with the many blessings I have.

Music is a universal, and there is nothing like listening to some great music when you are happy or sad, crying or laughing, or just sitting and soaking. It is always a good time to sing!

Finally, everybody needs somebody to talk to. There is nothing like a friend. You can share with a friend. You can find help in a friend. A friend can be a calming voice in your life.

Life always brings its challenges, and it is completely up to us how we navigate them. Make the decision to journey through this life with a smile on your face. Happiness is a choice.

Being happy is not dependent on what you have or do not have. Be happy with what you do have. Happiness is not based on anything external. It is generated internally. You make a decision to be happy. Being happy with what you have leads to gratefulness, and that leads to thankfulness, and that is what will ultimately generate more happiness.

What is your word?

Pick your song.

Tell your friends what they mean to you.

Trust People until They Give You a Reason Not To

We are only trusted with something when someone believes in our character. Being trusted with anything is a position of stewardship. We are being asked to steward something that is important to someone else. To be known as a good steward means someone believes in your capabilities.

I have worked with several organizations over the years, and I have had leaders say to me, "My employees have to earn my trust." My response is always, "They should not have to earn your trust. As a leader, you should give it first. If you want your employees to be trustworthy, show them how trustworthy you are. If they have to earn your trust, they should not work for you. Why would you hire someone you do not trust?"

When you give trust, you receive trust, not the other way around. Maybe, like me, you have heard someone say, "I am not very trusting." It is really a shame because they are probably not going to be trusted much by other people. Relationships are built on trust, and these people will certainly lack in meaningful relationships.

Sometimes when we do not trust people, it is an issue with us and not the individual we do not trust. We may have been burned by someone because we allowed ourselves to trust them. Do not let one individual's lack of trustworthiness get in the way of your trusting other people.

Showing trust empowers people. Empowered individuals are able to accomplish more. Trust is uplifting. People know if you just trust them on a casual level or if you trust them on a more significant, deeper level. People will respond to you based on the level of trust they feel. Trust is a firm belief in someone and their ability.

Write down what is in the way of your trusting people.

Trust in Yourself

We have an internal switch that tells us right from wrong and good from bad. You may have had a time when you resigned your position in your company not certain of what was to come, but you knew it was the right thing to do. Shortly after, you found yourself in your dream job.

Sometimes we do not always know what the next step is; we simply know we have to take a step. The only thing we have to go on is a feeling and our gut instinct. Many times we talk ourselves out of something great for us out of fear, not trusting that internal knowledge.

Taking the next step is a decision. Sometimes we fight making decisions, but doing so will always hold us back and deny us of our potential. See your decision to move forward as a decision to go on an adventure. We may not know where we are going to end up, but life offers so many positive possibilities that I choose to believe that where we end up will be great.

I have always found that in my gut, I knew what was the right thing to do. I did not always listen, however. Afterward, I would think to myself that I should have listened; I should have trusted myself. Trusting yourself is a learned behavior and is reinforced over time. You have everything you need to be successful. Trust that you are ready.

I believe we all have unique talents and gifts, but the one that we all have in common is the ability to trust ourselves when we have taken the time to really know who we are. This is not a one-time event. It is a process of consistently living your values, and sometimes that is not easy. But a commitment to the process will shape you, and you will trust your decisions.

Do you have confidence in your abilities? Do you trust yourself to make a decision? When you believe in yourself and your ability, you develop a trust that can move you forward. Trusting yourself means that your belief in yourself is beyond question. This absolute belief in yourself builds the foundation for you to trust others.

Take two minutes and write down your thoughts after reading the previous page.

Keep Your Commitments

The whole power of a nonnegotiable arises from its being a standard that you take on and live out in your personal life first and then extend into your business life. It is not the other way around. It is a standard by which you measure every decision—and never waver.

I have observed people who maintain the highest standards of integrity and those who vacillate and are not the same at the dinner table as they are at the board table—and the difference is evident in their success. The difference is evident in their relationships as well.

Someone who lives his or her nonnegotiables and never wavers always attracts people to them. They are admired for their strength of character. They build relationships and grow their personal and professional networks.

Even when we use universal terms like "standards" and "commitments," people still interpret them differently. To help us understand the true meaning I am conveying, consider the following three levels of commitment to our standards.

THE LOWEST LEVEL OF COMMITMENT TO OUR STANDARDS IS THE OPINION

For instance, consider the commitment "Do what's right." We could also say, "I do what is right." We could phrase it in any number of ways. But no matter how we choose to say it, at the lowest level, we do not yet have any action to serve as evidence that we mean it. It is all talk. There has only been verbal expression without any tangible action on our part in support of the opinion that we have shared. We have not yet done anything in support of the value. As a result, we have not yet set a nonnegotiable.

THE NEXT LEVEL OF COMMITMENT TO OUR STANDARDS IS THE ACTION

At this level, we have taken some kind of conscious action, however small, in support of keeping our word. So if we have done what is right on purpose, even one single time, then we have moved up to this second level. It is not just an opinion anymore. We can defend our opinion based on evidence. The trouble is, at this point, our actions are not always consistent. That is, we may not take actions that support our words all the time. For instance, we may only support our words with actions when it is easy or popular to do so. We still have not identified a nonnegotiable.

THE THIRD LEVEL OF COMMITMENT TO OUR STANDARDS IS THE NONNEGOTIABLE

At this level, we have made a decision to take a stand in support of our opinion and our belief, even though it might be easier to do something else. In other words, we hold the line when it is unpopular or difficult to do so. We take a stand and make the standard "Do what's right" something that is unyielding in our life. It is something internal, something we own, an outcome we can and do control. Whenever we decide something is an absolute in our life and then live it out as a nonnegotiable, we control that aspect of our life.

An opinion or an action only becomes a nonnegotiable once we actually take a stand for it when it would be easier not to. Just talking about the standard is not enough.

When you make a commitment to someone, do you keep it? When you make a commitment to yourself, do you keep it? A commitment is absolute and cannot be justified away. You keep a commitment no matter what. Do you fulfill all your obligations, both pleasant and unpleasant?

How do you keep rationalizations and justifications from getting in the way of keeping all your commitments?

Set Goals

We all have areas in our lives in which we want to improve, and one way to do that is to set a goal. Many times we set a goal for ourselves that we do not reach because it is too big or unobtainable and we become discouraged. When we become discouraged, we begin to think negative thoughts and our goals elude us. Discouragement causes us to quit and give up.

We are more likely to achieve our goals if we can think of them as the next step. The next step is always an incremental achievement on the way to a bigger event. So, if we take our goals and break them down into a number of next steps, we are more likely to reach our goals.

Next steps are smaller and, many times, do not require a lot of time to achieve. As we achieve our "next step" goals, we continue to move forward, we reinforce a belief in our abilities, and we gain momentum. Just like a toddler who is learning to walk doesn't just stand up one day and start running but rather begins by pulling himself up on furniture and cruising alongside it and then eventually lets go, we simply need to keep our eye on the next thing to do and we will soon reach our goal.

Goals are the targets of life. They add purpose and meaning to everything we do. Without them, you will go through each day without direction. Goals help keep us focused on what we say is most important to us. With goals, you supercharge every minute and every hour of your day.

Goals lead to superior planning and results. However, creating a vision toward which we are striving does not mean we must be bound to it every step of the way. Do not be afraid to reevaluate your goals and intentions along the way. Remember, very specifically written goals become magnets to which you will find yourself uncontrollably attracted.

What are your goals?

What are your goals for the next thirty days? Ninety days?

What are your goals for the next year? Three years?

Show Gratitude

Gratitude is one of those things that will always come back to you. To be grateful for the people you know is powerful, but the question is, can you be grateful for the people you do not know?

Are you grateful for the person who sacks your groceries? Are you grateful for the bank teller? Do you thank the waitress every time she fills up your tea glass?

Gratitude can even extend to people we may not have met. Are you grateful for the person who fed the chicken you are having for dinner? Are you grateful for the person who paved the road you drive on to get home? Are you grateful for the people whose names you don't even know but who have done something that has made your life better? Simple gratitude can and will make a difference in someone's life.

I find that the people who show the most gratitude in their life are the ones who believe that much has been given to them. When people think they have earned everything themselves, they tend to want to hold on to it tightly and they rarely show thanks to anyone. When we believe that good events have happened because of our hard work and the hard work of others and that much has been given to us, we learn to be thankful and look to share more with others. We are thankful for the physical things that have come our way, and more importantly, we are thankful for the people in our lives and the people we may not know but who, we understand, have played a part in what we enjoy.

When we are grateful, peace becomes a part of our lives. The power of gratitude keeps us in a place where we have our minds on other people. Gratitude is a positive conscious thought that will produce positive conscious actions—but only if it is real.

True authentic gratitude elicits the best from others. When you are gracious to others, not only are you appreciative of their service, but you are encouraging them to continue to be the best they can be to the people in their life. Know the source of all your gifts and show gratitude.

Who is the source of your gifts?

Accept Responsibility

Responsibility is not something that should be taken lightly. If you have been given any responsibility in your job, you have been given a certain amount of trust. When someone gives you trust, you want to reward that trust by showing up, getting the job done, and being dependable.

When we are given responsibility and we accept it, we begin a process where we are able to show what we are capable of doing. If we show we have the ability to take on additional responsibility, we are more likely to be promoted in our jobs. Responsibility is what we teach our children, and it is how they grow and become successful. Responsibility is the first step in making things right when we have done something wrong.

Leaders understand that they have many responsibilities. Ultimately, they know that the responsibility for the success or failure of the people and the organization always comes back to them. Leaders never deflect responsibility. They embrace it.

Accepting responsibility is a noble act. It is an act of honor. It is an act of leadership. If you are known as a responsible individual, people will see you as trustworthy. When this happens, it leads to more responsibility in your job, your family, or your community.

Are you always looking for shortcuts? Do you believe that others are luckier than you? Is there a magic formula for the success you are seeking? Future results are based on present actions. You are responsible for your actions and, therefore, your results. Taking responsibility for your success is the first step on the road to excellence.

What does it mean to be responsible?

Remove Negativity from Your Life

A friend of mine was diagnosed with stage 5 chronic kidney disease and found out she needed a kidney transplant. As she is waiting on her transplant, she has had to begin the process of dialysis. We were having a conversation one day, and she told me that she was struck by how sad the other patients seem to be who are on dialysis and she was determined to find a way to make a difference.

In her new normal of going to dialysis three times a week, she decided that what she could do is go a few minutes early and say hi to everyone and just give them a smile. I was deeply moved by her willingness to spread her positive energy when she herself was walking through her own challenges.

You see, we all get to choose our attitude and our approach to life. We can choose to be offended. We can choose to be greedy. We can choose to be negative. Or, we can choose to be grateful. We can choose to be happy. We can choose to be positive. We all have that choice. We just need to be mindful of our thoughts and how we choose to feel.

Negative thinking leads to negative results. When we think the worst, many times that is just what happens. We are so busy being negative that we fail to see the challenges, understand the opportunities, and make the decisions that will lead us to a positive result.

Negative thinking also repels others. Who wants to hang out with a negative person?

In our jobs and personal lives, there will be trials and tribulations, tough times and tougher times. But we have control over whether we approach those circumstances with a negative attitude or a positive attitude.

Do you bathe yourself with negative thoughts? Are you negative to those around you? Do you find yourself surrounded by others who insist on being negative about either their lives or yours? Negative attitudes and statements drain your life's energy. Each negative statement, by either yourself or someone else, draws energy from you. Energy is critical to work and production. Reduce or eliminate your negative thoughts, and work to surround yourself with people who are positive and give you energy rather than those who are negative and take your energy.

How do you remove negativity from your life?

Use Change as an Avenue to Growth

In the classic movie *The Wizard of Oz,* Dorothy and her gang believe the wizard to be a powerful man. His voice alone causes them to fear him. But when the curtain is pulled back, the wizard is revealed to be the powerless noisemaker that he is.

Change is much like the wizard. It really does not have any power unless we give it power. I know that many times I have heard people say, "I hate change." Just this negative way of thinking stymies these people in their personal lives and at work. These people do not realize that they have endured great, positive, and powerful changes in their life. They do not realize that anything good that they have experienced has come about by some sort of change. Graduating from school is change. Getting married is change. Having children is change. There are many wonderful times in our lives that come about as a result of change.

Change happens all the time. It happens every time a new employee joins the team or an organization gets a new client.

Sometimes in our organizations when we find out something is changing the only thing that has really happened is that a decision has been made. Do not let change throw you for a loop. You have control over how you approach it. Embrace change and the opportunities it brings.

Change is the essence of progress. Change is a gift and an opportunity. Through change, you have the opportunity to grow and prosper. Sameness is the enemy of us all. Resisting change is negative. It derails your focus and drains your energy.

Real change does not start with just modifying your actions, your methods, or your systems. Real change is a result of altering what you believe about a situation. When you change what you believe, that will drive you to change what you do. This change in action is permanent and sustainable.

By tapping into your creative powers and embracing change, you envelope yourself with a force that will foster and nourish your growth. It is not just about changing what you do. Change in any area always starts with transforming what you believe. When you change what you believe, you will change your actions and receive a different result.

How do you react to change?

Stand Up for Your Convictions and Beliefs

Standing up for your convictions and beliefs is not about you being right and everybody else being wrong. When you stand for something, people tend to trust you more because they know your word is your bond. They may not agree with you, but they respect you for taking a stand.

Just because you have strong convictions and beliefs does not mean you are not willing to hear another's point of view, but it does mean you are certain of what you believe and value.

Oftentimes people do not want to take a stand because they are afraid of what people will think and say. When you do this, you diminish your value as an individual. Other times people do not take a stand because they have never taken the time to know what they believe and value. Your beliefs and values shape your character. Your foundational beliefs are what help you determine what is right and wrong.

If you allow someone to say something that is wrong or do something that is inappropriate and you do not express yourself and stand up for your convictions and beliefs, then you are, in effect, supporting them. What you allow in your space you condone.

I used to hear someone say something that was sexist or racist and think to myself, "That is just wrong." I had a nice thought, but it did not change anything around me. I did not do anything. Now I speak up.

With respect, I point out that the comment someone just shared is sexist or racist or where it is wrong. Maybe they really believe that way. Maybe they just did not understand what they were saying. I express my beliefs in a way that allows them to realize the full meaning of their words and possibly retract or adjust their statement. Regardless, I let the people around me know that I do not agree with that way of thinking or acting and, ultimately, that I will not allow that kind of thinking to go on around me unchecked.

Do you know what you believe and value? How strong is your character? Are you able to stay your course when others around you condemn your ideas and display negativity? Can you live with what you want and what you believe is right even when it is not the popular view? Do you make your own decisions, or do you allow others to decide your fate for you?

How do you stand up for your beliefs and convictions?

How do you handle that moment when someone wants you to act contrary to your beliefs?

Live Your Life with Passion

Living your life with passion does not always mean you are having fun. When you have passion for what you do, you have an unquenchable desire to keep doing what you do no matter how hard it gets. Passion drives you to keep moving forward.

When we think of the word *passion*, rarely do we think of its first meaning, which is "suffering." We naturally think of something that makes us feel good and comfortable. The truth is, if you have passion for something, you are willing to suffer for it. Passion is powerful and painful. People with passion keep going no matter how painful it is to do so, no matter how complicated it is, and no matter who gets in the way. If you are truly living your life with passion, then you have pushed through the suffering and come out on the other side.

I love to write. I love to share ideas that can make a difference. Writing books and speaking to groups is a passion for me. Writing this book took time and energy. There were many days when I would have liked to be doing one thing, but I knew that I committed to a deadline with my publisher. What made writing this book possible was that I am passionate about what I do. Yes, some days it might be more fun to go to a ball game or take a hike, but my passion for sharing my message drives me forward.

Passion is an emotion that is highly contagious. Your passion will fuel other people's passion, and in our organizations this is where creativity takes place. Passion is the fuel for any cause. It is the energy for any mission.

Passion is the seed of discovering your purpose. It is the foundation for every accomplishment. Passion fuels desire. Your level of passion will dictate your level of success. Passion is unyielding, ever flowing, and always available to call upon.

What are you passionate about?

How do you show it?

Have Patience

Raising four kids who are all very different, you learn what it means when they say, "Patience is a virtue." If you interact with people in any way, patience is something that must be learned.

When I find myself exhibiting a lack of patience, it is usually with people who may not do things the way I would do them. Through the years I have had to learn that just because someone does something differently does not mean they are doing it wrong. It is wrong to judge people based on how they do something, and I work hard to consciously remember that.

I have also discovered that when I lose my patience, it is often because I am focused solely on me and ignoring that other people have needs also.

It is easy to be impatient with people. That commonly happens when we are driving. The truth is that we do not know why someone is acting the way they act or doing what they are doing. We do not know their story, their situation, and the challenges they may be facing. Having patience is a gift that we give others and that we give ourselves. Patience produces contentment and satisfaction in our lives.

It takes a certain amount of time for a cake to rise. Rushing the process will only ruin the cake. Patience does not mean not caring.

It means taking an appropriate action while understanding that the process takes time.

Patience means allowing the necessary amount of time to pass in order for natural events to mature and success to happen. It does not mean not pushing ahead with vigor. It just means you realize that there can be a set of steps you must pass through as you move to the top.

How do you balance your drive for results with patience?

In what situations could you be more patient?

With whom in your life could you have more patience?

Be Compassionate

If you are an individual filled with compassion, you will always be moved to do something. Compassion is felt first, and its power leads you to ask yourself the question, "What can I do?" And for people who have compassion, the answer is never, "Nothing."

Compassion drives action. Compassion is what started organizations like United Way, the Jewish Community Centers, the Salvation Army, homeless shelters, after-school programs for disadvantaged children, and countless other programs for people who need help.

Compassion does not care about the color of one's skin, their socioeconomic status, or what side of town they live on. Compassion only cares about one thing, and that one thing is "How can I help?"

Compassion always moves into action. It is that action that makes a difference in the lives of people. There can be no greater service than people helping people.

Everyone needs a hand now and then. Everyone appreciates a kind word. A genuine care for others translates into words and actions. People need to hear words of praise and see your feelings, as displayed in actions. Action on your part validates your words. Sincere concern, appreciation, and care are enormously empowering.

How do you show compassion?

Is compassion something that consistently shows up in your life?

Learn from Others

I do not believe in coincidences. I believe that when I meet someone it is for a reason. In that moment, maybe I am supposed to teach them something, or maybe they are supposed to teach me something, or maybe it is both.

By believing this, I am always asking myself the questions, "Why have we been brought together? What can I share with this person? What can I learn from them and this situation?"

Everyone has a story, and so often we just blow through our lives never taking the time to learn and enjoy all the interesting people who are in our lives and cross our paths.

Many times we think we can learn only from someone who is rich, someone who has an advanced degree, or someone who is in a position of power. The truth is that we can learn from all people. I have had conversations with people on the street corner and came away having learned something about attitude, life's perspectives, and even politics.

As the founder of the Accountability Movement, I have been blessed with the opportunity to talk to many people. Recently, I conducted a series of conversations with groups of people of different ages, races, socioeconomic status, and religions. Some of them I had met, but most of them I was meeting for the first time. We talked about religion, race, politics, business, education, and a multitude of other subjects. I learned from them, they learned from me, and we learned about life together.

Vicarious learning, learning from others' experiences, is the least expensive way to learn anything. Learning from someone who has achieved the results you desire will greatly shorten your learning curve and increase your staying power as you move toward your goals.

What gets in the way of your learning from other people?

Do you give credit to those people from whom you have learned?

Stay Focused

Focus is a commonly used word in the English language, but I think the true depth of its meaning gets lost at times. In the *Webster's 1828 Dictionary*, the word *focus* is defined as "a point of concentration."[1]

Professional athletes are able to focus with precision. During a game there are plenty of distractions going on all around them. The other team is trying to distract them. The fans may be yelling for them or against them. The coaches on the sidelines are shouting instructions. And the venders are trying to sell their wares in the stands.

Yet with complete accuracy, a basketball player is able to hit a three-point basket with nothing but net, or a quarterback can put the ball in the hands of a receiver 60 yards down the field. They do not eliminate the distractions; they are able to focus in spite of them.

One of the most important things we can do for ourselves is to know what the distractions are in our life. Just as with the professional athlete, we may not be able to eliminate the distractions from our lives, but we can learn to focus in spite of them.

---

1 *Webster's 1828 Dictionary* (1828), s.v. "focus," http://webstersdictionary1828.com/Dictionary/focus.

Some distractions come in the form of noise, such as the fans in the stands. Some distractions come in the form of opportunities, which, while they may look good, are not the right opportunities for you. Sifting through the barrage of distractions that will naturally come our way is part of the process.

I am an idea guy. I am constantly coming up with new ideas about how to do something or a way to do something better. The problem is the ideas might not always align with my mission and vision. I have to work hard to stay focused. I have to remember that even though it may be a good idea, if it is not in line with my focus, it is not a good idea for me.

Additionally, I love gadgets and technology. Sometimes I get too focused on the newest releases. This is a hobby for me. Some people like to fish. Some like to read. Others like to paint. We all have hobbies. It is important to embrace our hobbies but not let them distract us from our focus.

Is there order to your actions? Can you decide what is most important, somewhat important, and unimportant as you focus on your goals? Do distractions get in the way of critical activities and goals? Do you take care of the significant issues in your life so that you can move on to less meaningful ones?

Focus adds power to your actions and greatly enhances your ability to achieve at a very high level. Once you have focused on what you want to accomplish, your thoughts and actions should be like a laser beam on what you need to make it happen. Focus means you are able to hit the shot despite the distractions.

In what areas of your life do you need greater focus?

In what areas do you need to refocus?

Are there areas in your life that need less focus?

Laugh

At times we find ourselves going to the doctor for something that is wrong with us, and the doctor may find it necessary to prescribe us a medication. When this happens, we are told to take the medicine at a specific time of the day for a certain length of time. Usually at the end of the regimen we find ourselves healed and feeling 100 percent better.

Laughter is said to be medicine to the soul, and I believe we should do it every day as if a doctor has prescribed it to us to make us well. Laughter is contagious and has the power to make those around us feel better. Laughter binds us together in ways that make us feel comfortable with each other, and it gives us the ability to communicate on a more informal level.

There are experts who laud the benefits of laughter in life and in business. There are scientists who study laughter. Studies show that laughter is so powerful that it affects the whole body when we do it. Science tells us that when we laugh, the T-cells in our immune system are increased, which is the body's natural defense against diseases. Laughter really is a medicine!

Do you laugh? When? How seriously do you take yourself? Can you laugh at past mistakes? Laughter is therapeutic. Laughter releases endorphins in your body. It makes you feel good. When you feel good, others around you feel good.

Find things to laugh at. Look for the humor in everyday situations. Live a life filled with laughter. And, you will find, laughter is contagious.

Are there situations where you take yourself too seriously?

How can you bring more laughter into your life and the life of others around you?

Listen to Others

I heard a story about a man who was suffering from a debilitating muscular disease that affected every muscle in his body. At times the disease would cause his voice to become nothing more than a faint whisper.

This gentleman went to a birthday party for kids in the foster care system, and he struck up a conversation with a ten-year-old girl. As luck would have it, this was a day when his voice was barely audible, making it impossible to hear what he was saying. The young girl was so determined to hear what he had to say that she got down on one knee and put her ear up to his mouth in order to understand him, and they carried on a beautiful conversation.

That is what it looks like to listen. Listening means you are so determined to hear what the other person is saying that you are willing to do almost anything to understand.

Listening shows that you care about the other person, you care about their opinions, and you care about their feelings. Listening is a way of honoring someone. Listening is a way of learning from other people. Ultimately, when you show an interest and listen, you are positioned to build more meaningful relationships.

Do you learn more from speaking or listening? Do you control the conversation? Can you listen more than you talk? Do you express your opinion to satisfy your ego or to contribute to the conversation and move it toward solving issues and providing new information? Are you telling or learning?

When you listen, you learn about the other person, their interests, and their concerns. Listening positions you to serve more thoroughly and to respond better to the needs of other people. Listening is about trying to understand. Listening shows you care.

In every conversation you have for the next five days, make a specific effort to listen completely before offering your words and thoughts.

Pay the Price

One of my favorite things to do is to shop at the Apple store. I admit it. I am like a kid in a candy store! And if I go in the store, I am probably going to buy something.

Whenever I make the decision that I am going to purchase something, the first thing I do is decide what I am going to buy. The next thing I do is take the item to the counter and pay for it. Then the item belongs to me. It is mine to do whatever I want with it. I paid the price.

The items that really matter in life—and these are usually not going to be things but rather experiences and relationships—are going to cost us something. If we want to be the best in our careers, it is going to cost us something. To be at the top of your game probably means you have sacrificed something, and that is never easy. It takes time and commitment to be a great parent or to be a great child for an aging parent.

Everything you want to accomplish has a price attached to it. The price may be expressed in dollars, but usually it is expressed in time, energy, sacrifice, and commitment. Are you willing to pay the price for what you say is important to you? Making that commitment is the first step to moving forward on your goals.

Take the time to think about the price you need to pay for the goals you have. Count the cost.

It Is Your Decision

Making accountable decisions is not easy. If it were, everyone would do it. Accountability is keeping your commitments to people. You are responsible for things but accountable to people. Accountability always involves people and relationships. When we start thinking about ourselves and our own personal gain, we may find that we are not being accountable to the people around us.

I struggle daily with many of the thoughts and challenges that I have written about in this book. It is in my personal struggle and the sometimes-resulting pain that I find my answers and my growth. Personal growth is an initiative that never ends. It takes a continuous commitment to want to be better.

Good decisions are based on education, quality information, and a personal commitment to the positive outcome you desire. Success comes from defining the decisions you need to make, making those quality decisions, and then taking action on your decisions.

Positive results and success do not always show themselves at once. In fact, sometimes we must experience hardship and negative results in order to learn, build, and make better decisions. Failure only comes from quitting and denying the process the necessary time in order to evolve into success.

Every day you are faced with decisions. Where you end up in this world is up to you. You have the opportunity to shape your legacy. Your legacy is based on your vision, the way you think, and the decisions you make. Most times there is so much more that is available to us, but we do not realize it. It is available only if we make the conscious choice to be that person or pursue that endeavor. It is your decision.

Bonus Material

NO MATTER WHAT

Introduction

What Is a Commitment?

I am good with ideas. We all have strengths, and creating ideas is mine. I come up with ideas for my friends to utilize both personally and professionally, I formulate ideas that my clients can use in their organizations, and I create ideas that apply to my business. Over the years, I have formulated a lot of great ideas that have made a significant difference for the people around me and for myself.

When I look at the decisions I regret most in my personal or my professional life, I realize that I do not regret any decisions to try something new. What I regret is that I did not stick with some of those ideas. I regret not being committed to those ideas to the point of seeing them through to success. I honestly believe that I have given up on many ideas that, if I had been sincerely committed to them, could and should have led to significant success. It does sadden me to think of some of the opportunities I have missed out on because of a lack of commitment.

Today I am very careful about which creative ideas I take on. Just because something is a good idea does not mean that it is right for me. I know this and find that if I am selective in what I take on, my time and energy is focused, I am committed, and more often than not I achieve success. Having experienced the lack of positive outcomes that result from not being committed has taught me to be choosy in what I commit to and, when I do commit, to go all in and make it happen.

A Commitment Unleashes Power and Potential

There is a power that comes with commitment. What is that power? Power is a force you cannot see. It always produces, and it is 100 percent guaranteed. The power of commitment will not fail you. Whatever you are committed to will produce a result for you. The fact that you are committed creates positive results. That is the power.

The power of commitment is transformational. It can transform us, the people around us, our organizations, and even our world.

Commitment unleashes potential. It allows you to become your best. One of the greatest transformations that commitment produces is the development of your character.

A Commitment Involves Challenges and Sacrifices

Commitments are not easy. Your accountability will often be tested by challenges and conflicts: Are you going to keep your commitment even in the face of personal loss, in the midst of a crisis, or when it is not in your best interest to do so? A commitment has to do with character. Everyone is committed when it is easy, but when a conflict shows up so does the truth about whether or not you are committed. This is where your accountability is manifested. This is where your character is developed.

Just as a plant has to push through the earth to see the sun and grow, we too have to "push through" our challenges and conflicts and keep our commitments. It is in those moments that we grow as people. That blade of grass you see outside is pushing up through earth that is much heavier than itself. It is not easy. The plant goes through enormous stress to surface from the ground. Pushing through is not easy for plants, and it is not easy for us. Yes, we will have stress. Yes, we will have to work hard. And yes, we will be able to persevere and make it. In that moment that we overcome a difficulty to keep a commitment, we become something else—something better and something that will never go back.

Not only are commitments not easy; life is not easy. Anyone who achieves greatness and significance has made tremendous sacrifices. A sacrifice is serious. A sacrifice is not giving something up that is extra or unnecessary. It is giving up something important in order to do or achieve something that is of even greater significance.

We do not always see those sacrifices. We just see success on television or in the news and forget what went into it. That sacrifice always came because of some sort of commitment. The athlete committed to spending hours each day for years to develop his skill set. The doctor committed to spending hours each day for years learning about medicine. The entrepreneur with seemingly "overnight success" committed to spending years learning her trade and building a business in anonymity before achieving the success that we get to see.

A Commitment Is No Matter What

When we define accountability as "keeping one's commitments to people," it is easy to look past the word *commitment*. It is easy to think, "Oh yeah, I know what a commitment is. Everyone knows what a commitment is. It is when you say 'yes,' or 'I will,' or maybe even 'I do.'"

The reality is that people view commitments differently. Commitment is an incredibly powerful word. Without defining what a commitment is, we would undermine the definition of accountability.

A commitment is "No Matter What." Just because you hit tough times does not mean you need to move on or that it is time to quit. Just because something is hard does not mean you should do something else. Where is the commitment in that?

A commitment is "No Matter What."

A commitment is a pledge. It is a promise. It is not a maybe, or a hopefully, or a probably. It is an absolute. It is a No Matter What.

There is a seriousness in making a commitment. There is another level of commitment where it gets into your DNA, where you do not even think about the possibility of not doing it. This is the level of "No Matter What." This is the level that a true leader and accountable person reaches.

This definition of commitment will totally change the way you see everything. No Matter What™ has become my personal mantra. When you see everything through this lens, conviction takes on an entirely new meaning. What is possible expands because you are not going to give up along the way. Relationships are deepened because the people around you know that you have their back, always and every time. That is because it is a No Matter What!

There is a power that comes with a commitment.

When you take the position of No Matter What, you are not looking to hedge. You are all in. You will never be looking for a way out. You will only seek a way in. When you take the position of No Matter What, you develop a reputation for being reliable. Everyone around you knows where you stand in any situation. They know they can depend on you regardless of circumstances, and this frees them to focus on moving forward. When they know they can depend on you, you will discover that you can also depend on them. It becomes mutual.

In any situation and in any relationship, there are only three possible positions to take: *no*, *maybe*, and *yes*. *No* is obvious. *Maybe* means it is possible, but it also means it might not be possible or will not happen.

When our children were younger, they would ask my wife, Renee, if they could do something or if we could go somewhere. Sometimes the answer would be "yes" and sometimes the answer would be "no." Many times the answer was "maybe." "Maybe" meant the door was open but that it was not guaranteed. Actually, "maybe" was usually code for "I do not want to say 'no' so I am saying 'maybe,' but 'most likely' the answer will end up being 'no,' though it is still possible." Whew! Over time, when the kids heard Renee say, "Maybe," they came to learn what it meant and would respond, "Oh, that means 'no.'"

The real problem is when someone says, "Yes," but it really is a "maybe." This is not a commitment. This is someone who is not reliable. And over time people come to know that a "yes" from that person does not mean "yes." Because the person is not reliable, his or her credibility suffers. They lose the personal power that comes from a reputation of No Matter What.

Are you looking for a way out or are you looking for a way in?

Yes is a commitment, and a commitment is No Matter What. When you take this position, you will move heaven and earth to make it happen. This means your commitments make you a far more powerful individual, not only in the eyes of the people around you, but also in your actual ability to make something happen.

When people know you are committed to them, the power of a commitment grows even stronger. The people to whom you commit know that you believe in them, that you trust them, that you want them to succeed, and that you meet their needs before your own. This is the way an accountable person and a great leader operates.

Leaders are guarded with what they say. They think before they speak. When they do speak, what they say is based on what they believe and value. They do not just spout off randomly. They know what they are saying. A leader always remembers what they say. Part of commitment is being careful to remember what you say and agree to. Not remembering that you promised to do something is not an acceptable excuse for not doing it.

People who live *No Matter What* are guarded by what they say and are not "moved by the moment." They make their decisions and promises based on what they really believe, feel, and can deliver on.

A Commitment Requires Honesty and Transparency

Honesty and transparency are the core of keeping your commitments. In a work environment people do not easily commit to people they do not know and trust. Leaders get to know the people they lead and allow those people to get to know them in return. When leaders are transparent, you have the opportunity to get to know them. Do the people in your organization or in your life know you? Do they really know you?

Your belief in a cause or mission may be enough for you to sacrifice for people you are working to support or whose lives you are helping to improve. You give from your heart, and you want to make a difference. It does not matter that you do not know the specific people. You know the cause. You know the challenges they face. You know the difference in their lives that you can make.

But in an organization, you may not sacrifice for someone you do not know. And it is only when you know someone that you can care for him or her. The real key is that leaders always care for their people first!

An essential person in my organization is my assistant, Sharon. We have daily discussions on accountability both organizationally and personally. We study the subject, develop depth to our philosophies, work with clients to help leaders and their organizations, and write speeches. It has not always been smooth sailing. Early on, we did not really know how to communicate with each other. And by early on I am talking about for three-plus years. We were constantly at each other's throats. Sharon could not believe that I did not fire her, and I could not believe that she did not quit. It was that rough sometimes.

The thing is that we knew each other. We knew each other's families. We knew each other's values. We were both committed to building a more accountable world. Sharon was committed to me and my mission, and I was committed to her.

We worked through those tough years and have built a wonderful friendship and developed a powerful ability to work together as a result. I know that she would always be there for me, and I believe she feels the same way.

A Commitment Requires Consistency, Clarity, and Equality

When you have a track record of No Matter What, there is a consistency. Your actions are always consistent with your words. It is that consistency of No Matter What that becomes a significant part of the underpinning of your character.

To have a commitment there has to be clarity. You have to know what it is that you are really committing to. You have to know the impact and the importance of the commitment. It is moving when you commit to something meaningful and deliver on that commitment.

People commit because they want to be part of something positive. They want to be a part of something that is bigger than them. They have a desire to be better. They want to contribute to a relationship and the betterment of someone else.

Organizations have the ability to offer all of that through their values. Employees are expected to live out the values. Whatever the leader is willing to commit to the employees will commit to. It becomes a reciprocal commitment.

A commitment has to do with equality. It has to do with fairness. When you're talking about an accountable culture, it cannot be one-sided.

When we work with an organization, we always find that if people in that organization are not being accountable, the leader isn't being accountable in the first place. It always starts with that leader. We always look at what leadership might be doing or if there are challenges, flaws, or weaknesses in the leadership. The truth may hurt, but it is the truth. Once we find those things that can be improved upon within the leadership, leadership can make changes. If leadership will get better, their team will get better. Everything rises and falls on leadership.

Everything rises and falls on leadership.

Our best clients are those clients where the leader says, "I want to get better." And then they are consistent about sharing that knowledge with the people they lead. They are saying, "If I am better at the same time that my team is getting better, then we are getting better as an organization."

Like I said, if the leader commits, then everyone else is going to commit. Without commitment what do you have? You have uncertainty and instability. There is doubt and inconsistency. None of these things produce an environment in which people enjoy working or that fosters tremendous success.

Without commitment, people do not bond. Relationships are key to communication and success. The organizations with the best relationships will outperform their competition every time. People working together, helping each other, and having each other's backs creates a high-productivity environment. It also creates a place where people like to work, which leads to great customer service and exceptional performance. It will not be like this without a unilateral commitment to the company's values.

A Commitment Requires Courage

It takes courage to commit. People have a hard time with what is not known. When you make a commitment, you do not always know how it is going to play out. You do not know what obstacles will come up. You do not know what possible opportunities you may have to say "no" to in order to keep your commitment.

Commitments are not always safe.

People often worry about what they are going to have to give up when they commit.

A lot of people like to be safe, and commitment can be risky business. Ask people if they are doing their dream job, and most times the answer will be "no." This is because people tend to play it safe. Playing it safe is what holds people back. We are talking about risk, and people are usually risk averse. What they do not understand is that through the commitment they will receive far more than what they may give up.

Not committing is the easy way out. Not committing does not take fortitude. It does not take consistency. You do not have to pay a price in time, energy, or possible lost opportunity. You avoid the tough decisions when you do not commit. In taking the easy way out, you lose all opportunity for personal growth, development, and gain.

A Commitment Brings Freedom and Other Positive Qualities

At the level of No Matter What there is freedom. You are a slave to nothing and no one. The power that flows through you at the level of No Matter What allows you total freedom to follow your beliefs and do what you know to be right.

Positive qualities are produced in our lives when we commit. Those qualities are trust, respect, loyalty, credibility, influence, and accountability. In addition, we are able to build more meaningful relationships. Even friendship and love are produced when you are willing to commit.

If you would not want any of these traits in your life or in the organization at which you work, speak now or forever hold your peace. Exactly! Trust, respect, loyalty, and the other high-performance qualities allow us to operate at a high level in our lives and in our organizations. And we see people and companies all the time that lack in these areas. They are the people with whom we do not want to hang out and the companies at which we do not enjoy working or which we will not recommend to our friends and family.

A commitment is something you give. My commitment to you is not based on whether you keep your commitment to me. That would make my commitment conditional. My commitment is No Matter What!

This is not a tactical subject. This is not a way of doing. This is a way of thinking. It is permanent. It is absolute. Most people are looking for options. They are looking for an easy-out clause—an "in case something comes up." People want wiggle room, but it can't be that way.

Accountability is not a way of doing. Accountability is a way of thinking. Commitment is not a way of doing. Commitment is a way of thinking. A way of thinking will always produce a result, and when it comes to accountability and commitment that result is incredibly positive and unbelievably powerful.

A Commitment Requires Passion

In order for people to be committed to something they need to be inspired and passionate. They have to have a reason to commit.

The inspiration comes from the leader. Everything flows from the head. Whatever the head is committed to is going to impact the direction that the organization goes. Whatever the leader is consistent and steady with is the direction in which the organization will go.

Commitment is not a way of doing.
It is a way of thinking.

So, if the leader is wishy-washy, the organization will be wishy-washy. If the leader is focused, the organization will be focused. And what the leader focuses on the organization will focus on. If the leader focuses on his or her people, then the people will focus on people—people inside the organization as well as people outside the organization, such as clients and the community.

Not everyone is a leader. A person has to accept the responsibility of leadership to start to become a leader. Leaders are first and foremost responsible for the people they lead. That responsibility has to be accepted in order to be a leader.

The leader's passion is what helps create the inspiration in the people they lead. Leaders communicate their passion very well. That passion attracts people who are inspired and who become committed.

What's a No Matter What in your life? When you determine what that is, you gain clarity, and that allows you to focus on moving forward.

The power of commitment, *No Matter What,* will free you and empower you. *No Matter What* will change your life.

Bring Accountability to Your Organization

Contact Us

Sam Silverstein, Incorporated

121 Bellington Lane

St. Louis, Missouri 63141

info@SamSilverstein.com

(314) 878-9252

Fax: (314) 878-1970

To Order More Copies of *Making Accountable Decisions:*

www.samsilverstein.com

Follow Sam

www.twitter.com/samsilverstein

www.youtube.com/samsilverstein

www.linkedin.com/in/samsilverstein

About the Author

Sam Silverstein is founder and CEO of Sam Silverstein, Incorporated, an accountability think tank dedicated to helping companies create an organizational culture that prioritizes and inspires accountability. By helping organizations develop what they believe in, clarify their mission, and understand what is in their control, Sam works to make this a more accountable world. He is the author of several books, including *No More Excuses*, *Nonnegotiable*, *No Matter What*, *The Success Model*, and *The Lost Commandments*. He speaks internationally, having worked with teams of companies, government agencies, communities, and organizations both big and small, including Kraft Foods, Pfizer, the United States Air Force, and United Way. Sam is the past president of the National Speakers Association.